The Architecture of Despair

The Underground Homeless of New York City

The Tunnel

Margaret Morton

Yale University Press
New Haven/London

The Tunnel was supported in part by New York
Foundation for the Arts, The Catalogue Project.

Margaret Morton's project was supported in part
by a Graham Foundation Grant for Advanced
Studies in the Fine Arts; National Endowment
for the Arts, Visual Artist Fellowship Grant in
Photography; and New York State Council on the
Arts, Individual Artist Grant. The Cooper Union
School of Art provided technical support.

Printed in the United States of America.

Library of Congress Cataloging–in–Publication Data
Morton, Margaret.
The tunnel : The underground homeless of New
York City/Margaret Morton
p. cm.– (The architecture of despair)
ISBN 0–300–06538–8 (cloth : alk. paper)
ISBN 0–300–06559–0 (pbk. : alk. paper)
1. Homeless persons–New York (N.Y.)–Case studies.
2. Homelessness–New York (N.Y.)–Case studies.
3. Squatters–New York (N.Y.)–Case studies.
4. Railroad tunnels–New York (N.Y.)–Case studies.
I. Title. II. Series.
HV4506.N6M67 1995
305.5'69–dc20   95–4894 CIP

A catalogue record for this book is available from
the British Library. The paper in this book meets
the guidelines for permanence and durability of
the Committee on Production Guidelines for Book
Longevity of the Council on Library Resources.

10 9 8 7 6 5 4 3 2 1

*This book is dedicated to those homeless individuals
who are rebuilding their lives beneath the streets of New York City.*

Contents

Prologue

The mud flats along the Hudson River were occupied by squatters when the Hudson River Railroad arrived in the mid–1800s. By the early 1900s both the homeless community and the railroad had expanded: a tar paper shantytown with 125 occupants lined the four tracks of the New York Central and Hudson River Railroad where it stretched six miles along an area known as Riverside Park.

Residents of the two dozen shanties scavenged food from mounds of garbage deposited there by the Sanitation Department. With the onset of the Great Depression, they were joined by starving crowds who set upon each new load of refuse before it was transported by scows to open sea.

In 1934 Robert Moses succeeded in his ambitious plan to transform the mud flats into a promenade for residents of the stately apartment houses perched on the overlooking bluff. The garbage dumping ceased, and the shantytown was cleared. The tracks, along with the dirt of the dense black smoke of the diesel engines and the odor of carloads of pigs and cattle en route to slaughterhouses, were concealed in a concrete structure topped with steel frames and buried beneath a landscaped fill that extended Riverside Park to the water. This tunnel, stretching 2½ miles from 72d Street to 123d Street, also provided shelter for assembly of the long diesel–pulled trains and at the widest sections accommodated clusters of concrete rooms designed for use by railroad personnel.

By the mid–1970s dramatic shifts had occurred in patterns of manufacturing and shipping. The railroad's West Side line, once the major entrance point for goods from the northern and western United States, was no longer profitable and rail service was discontinued. In 1991 Amtrak crews laying new track for passenger service from Penn Station to Albany discovered a community of more than 50 people living in the abandoned tunnel.

The north gate

June 7th, 1985, was the official day I first came to the abandoned train tunnel to dwell. My initial decision to live there was based on the fact that where I was at the time, which was an abandoned van underneath the 96th Street bridge, was taken away by Transportation, so we set up a tent in the park. For two weeks it rained practically everyday, and we were getting harassed by the Parks Department, so I told this guy that I met at the bathroom that we all were staying at that I knew of this train tunnel that looked abandoned. Bill and I decided to investigate, so we descended the stairs and something inside just told me to go left.

So we just started going left about maybe five or six hundred yards, and we saw some of these houses, and that was it. I said, "We'll get us some shelter, and we'll just go from there." And that was the beginning of something with me, as unique as it is. And till this day I still say it's probably the greatest thing that I've done in my life—it is.

Bernard

I have no regrets. I didn't plan on it going into [ten] years but that's the way life is. You make no plans sometimes. In most cases our decisions are to make more money, to acquire more things, material things and what. This existence has done so much for me. It's taken me from the vanity. I was just amazed at how I adapted to it, because I had lived right at 95th and Columbus for four and a half years — this same neighborhood. I had lived on the West Side for twelve years, and for me to be in my neighborhood and just to adapt to the lifestyle of a homeless person… It's been remarkable that I have done it with no shame. I've come in contact with some of the people that I have known over the years, prominent people in society — restaurant owners, producers, and choreographers — and they have been an inspiration to me because they say to me, "Well, your look is very different 'cause you used to be very well groomed, a very flashy dresser. And now I'm looking at a different person, but I can see that you are the same person." And I say, "Well, I guess I've been taught humility."

People think it's about laying back and being shiftless out here and it's not. A day–to–day existence can be most intense. There's a three–hour period that's probably more intense than the eight–hour workday for a person, and that's the three hours probably between one and four o'clock—sometimes it's later. I got up at five o'clock this morning. And that time is spent acquiring things. I usually run out to D'Agostino's. I love grapes. When they package grapes—all the grapes that fall off in the crates—they usually just discard them. So, I used to just come by and get four or five crates and just dump them all into one bag, and I'd have me three or four pounds of grapes. It's incredible. I mean, why should I go and pay a dollar ninety–nine for a pound for them—I can just go by and get all I want for free.

The other night I was coming by Food Emporium on 90th and Broadway—something just told me, "Take a peek in the dumpster," because it just come out. And I opened up the lid and I uncovered four cans of salmon and lobster bisque, fresh broccoli, carrots—had boxes of cookies. I mean, it was incredible stuff. I just took all the cans of salmon bisque, took two packs of cookies. And from there I walked up to the Korean vegetable stand. I mean food really is our least problem here—it's just that one must not have that false pride when it comes to going and getting.

I have always done most of the cooking. In most cases, people will heat up stuff down there. But cooking stews, soups—I'm an excellent cook. I love to cook. People say, "That was amazing!" I've never cooked professionally, I've never had a job as a cook. They thought I was in the military or something, which I wasn't.

Larry and I sat here the other day, and I made steamed cauliflower, wild rice, chicken. We're sittin' there listening to jazz—and a forty ounce of beer apiece. So we finished eating and he sat his feet on that side and I had my feet up here. And I said, "Larry, this is too simple for most people." See, people think they gotta be out there, out there chasing the next hit of crack or whatever. You can bring everything you want to do right here. You have your food. When this is over with, you go to bed. Your days—what more could you ask for? That's it.

My old room was the second house. The campsite was clear so we set up a grill there. I always wanted to be near where I had to come out to cook. I always liked that room, it was a big space. It measured 15 x 25 feet. A guy who lived down with me, his name was Nat, from South Carolina. I called him my homeboy 'cause I was born in South Carolina. I had this argument with Nat one morning. It's funny. This was a Monday morning. Nat's room had caught on fire that Sunday, and he was in Bob's room and, I don't know, he decided he was leaving, and he just took this vengeance. He was gonna do the only thing he figured could hurt me, which was to set my room on fire.

I slept in between Bob's room and Tony's room—it was an empty room. I slept there one night. Then I said to Don, "Don, help me put together the room next door to mine." Bob had left it, got grand, he'd started working at We Can and he left the room. So Donald helped me put the room together. And Donald and I lived in there for a month or two together, and Donald took my old room. He and Paul cleaned it out inside…so I let them have it. Didn't matter to me.

I had two big Persian rugs. They were about 5 x 10 feet. And the furnishings were a bed, a dresser. I just had wicker furniture. It was bad. Was very comfortable. Was like, when you got in there and you looked and you say, "Wow! I can't believe this is where a homeless person was set up." Everyone was really impressed by John at the south end's room. They always talked about [it] but they didn't understand. These rooms could be made… You could be livin' as comfortable as you chose. You could be as fabulous, as elaborate as you wanted it to be. Depends about how much time you want to put into it because the furnishings are unlimited out here on the streets. I mean, you walk and you find… Oh, my God, it's unbelievable.

It's funny how can redemption came to me. I remember as a kid in Florida I used to redeem bottles. My father and I had this heated discussion about my decision to live as I live, and he goes into, "You can be anything you want. You can go out and get any job you want—do something. Be self–sufficient, even if you have to collect cans for a living." Ha! So I went to the stores and investigated everything. I had to find what brands they took. And I was the first guy on this West Side, to my knowledge, that was doing it. Outside of the customers, the patrons of the store redeeming what they [bought]—I was the first guy going around. I had battles from 110th Street all the way down to 72d Street with the store owners. They wanted to restrict me.

This West Side is a gold mine. Thursday is my biggest day. Tuesdays, Wednesdays, and Thursdays. Fridays, there are certain spots I go by that I know the cans will be out and I'll just be there. On Tuesdays, I have two supers out here. I help them bring the papers and containers out, I get the cans. To [the can and bottle redemption center], you're talking a distance of maybe fifty–one blocks from 103d Street, and you're talking loaded with glass bottles. That's a lot of weight.

Can redemption is probably the greatest thing that ever happened to the City in a long time. You go to We Can one day and you'll see that it's not just homeless people. I mean you have a lot of elderly people, people on fixed incomes. It helps. It helps keep everything going.

I walk up to the gas station to get water. I've really missed the well. We had a waterline that was cut on the east wall of the tunnel, around 85th Street. I discovered it my first month down there, but I never used it because I thought it was runoff or sewage water. I would always take the catwalk on my route to go to All Angels Church, where I cooked for twenty months—Tuesdays, Thursdays, and Sundays. And one morning, what happened was, they'd shut all the water off in the parks because it was getting cold. And I was starting to worry where was I gonna get water from because going back and forth to the gas station was a little strenuous. And I said, "Would you look at this." So I put my light on the water, and I didn't see flies. And you could see clear to the bottom 'cause it drains off to the Hudson. And I stuck my hand in it. Smelled it—didn't smell. I tasted some. I said, "That's it. This definitely is a blessing." And I saw bars of soap around, and so people were coming down at the other end of the tunnel from the topside and they were taking baths down there. The most amazing thing about it—the water didn't freeze in the wintertime, the water just flowed effortlessly. And I started calling it the Tears of Allah. And that was a heartbreaker. When they started renovating the tunnel in '89, late '89 early '90, they shut it off. I think it was done purposely to deter us from being there, but it didn't stop anything…

I have a few people down every Friday night, usually get smoked up and drink some beer. It's very easy to get carried away at this level with the pleasures. The abuse of substances—alcohol, crack—those are pretty common at this level. I speak as an authority when it comes to the use and abuse of cocaine because I've been there and I know the ins and outs. Crack is really a fool's drug. It is. It is designed to create chaos. I had never smoked crack when I first came to the tunnel. But with crack and the tunnel—it was a haven for people to come and smoke in peace. I've got a canister, two canisters. I got maybe four or five thousand empty crack vials over the years. And it was always a reminder. It created so much chaos down there for me.

It was crazy, crazy—couldn't get no rest for a while because there was so much crack coming through. It was unbelievable. It was chaos, 'cause nothing was getting done. And the entire camaraderie down there—all of a sudden, it was based upon who could buy the next hit. The environment was suffering. People were not on top of water and it was costing me. I would go out to get something, and it's all been eaten up because someone thought they had the right to have it. And it was getting on my nerves—that's just going too far. It was bullshit, and I decided to eliminate everything, so it was denied. The people that were destructive with it—they left.

When something becomes chaotic, when something creates disturbance within your environment, it doesn't belong. When the environment suffers, changes have to be made. It's that simple.

Once the weather really breaks and gets warm, certain seeds will drop through the grate from up top and things sprout over there. That area has always had plant life. We had some tomato plants. I had a couple of fruit trees, but I really didn't protect them in the wintertime, and they died. It was amazing—some citrus plant that came up. It was either an orange or lemon tree. And the thing survived up until the middle of December. The first heavy snowstorm just killed it, but it blew my mind. But it will be very interesting to see what comes up for this spring. I guess you saw some of the melon seeds over there. I always throw the melon seeds of the watermelon, and they sprout and the vines will grow down the hill. And they always end up dying, but whatever. It's just good to see something green over there. That's why I do it all the time.

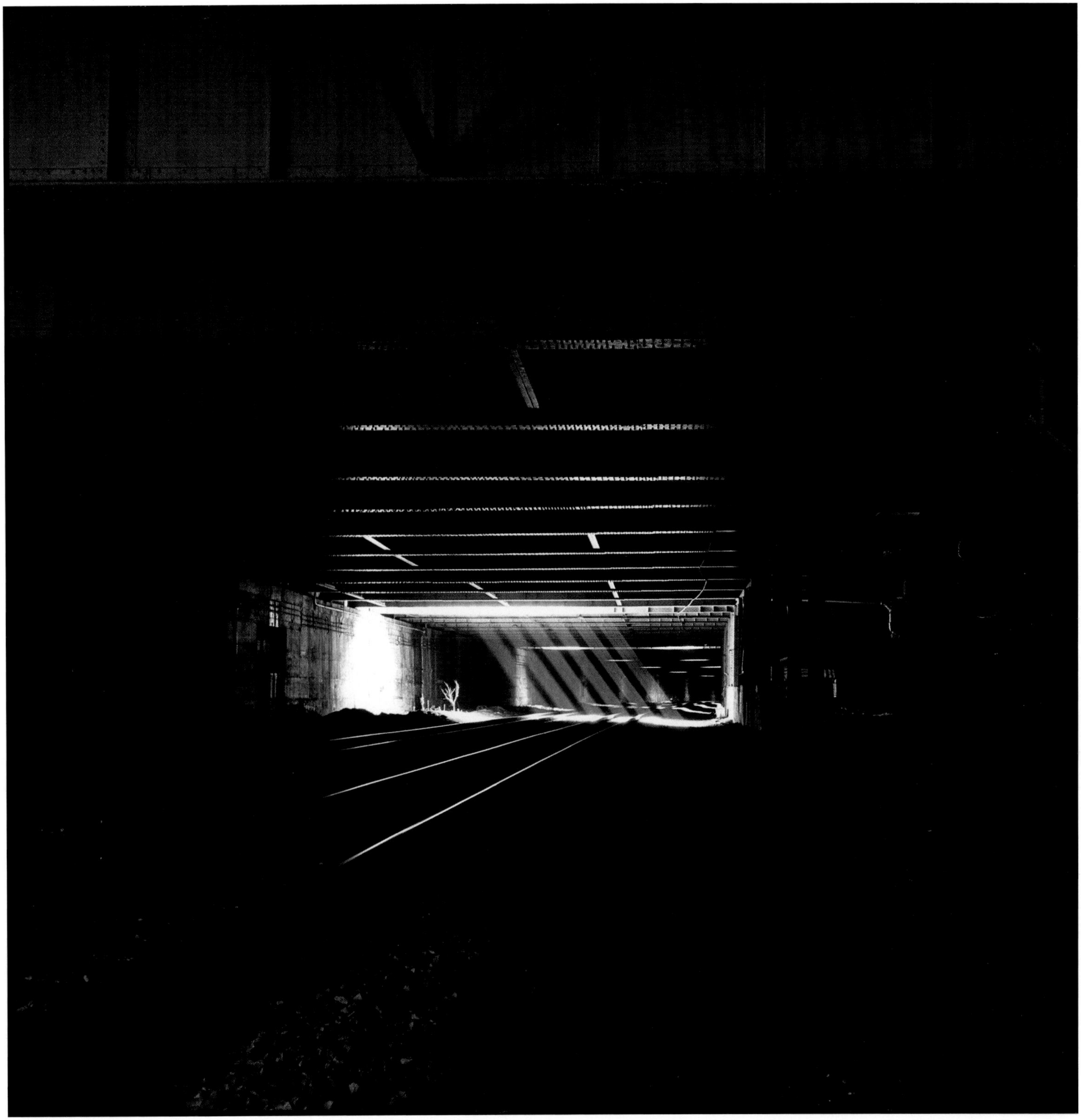

I envisioned that when I leave here that I was gonna leave something behind. I was eating a pear last week, and it was very ripe. And I tore it open and there was a seed part, and so I took the hole, like a cavity, and dug it out. And I planted the hole part right in the ground. I hope it grows. I'd like to leave something like a plant or tree behind and one day probably return here and say, "Wow, my tree has grown." That would be great to see.

There's a certain level of consciousness required of man. And one can't perfect that within functional society. You have to basically be separated and apart from it. And I guess that's why I'm going through what I'm going through. I've been put into a hell of an environment to try and perfect this. But by the same token, it's a perfect environment. It's all about one's focus and one's will to be. And everything is challenging.

Once my original roommate left, it was seventeen months of solitude. I mean I had a routine—had things to keep me busy—but I guess I was searching for that period where I would just totally be alone. And winter, when wintertime came, it gave me that. That's what I loved about winter because the tunnel was less active. And I figured if I was ever to touch base with that consciousness, it would be during that time period when I was totally isolated and the elements were in my favor to keep everyone away. And I don't know, for some reason it was interrupted. All these people came in and I guess it was a test of my tolerance. But I don't think that it's lost—what I was seeking—when one transcends into that other level.

I came to the belief that maybe I was being chastised for the seventeen months that I was there and didn't perfect something. I guess I wasn't prepared to. But this is my penitence, I guess, but I'll bear it. I'll accept it 'cause it will all come to an end.

Bob

The Amtrak Tunnel was built in about the 1930s over in Riverside Park. I met a fellow by the name of Bernard. One day I volunteered —volunteered cooking at a place called All Angels. Bernard and I got along okay and so he said, "If you ever need a place, come on down." Well this is about 1987, '86. I gave up all the wintertime for Bernard 'cause I moved into the tunnel.

I was born December 1, 1941. I was one of six children in the family. Three died at birth and I have two brothers. One's a priest and one's on the east [coast] Police Department. I was raised in a family where there was nothing but arguing. My parents argued every day of their marriage. They were married for fifty–two years. I was what you call a war baby. I was born seven days before Pearl Harbor. So for me it was like, "Here's money, do whatever you want, don't bother us." They said that I shouldn't have been born. I heard them say that. That was a mistake, and I left home at the age of sixteen. To this day —they're both dead—I've never seen my family, brothers or anybody since then.

I got married when I was seventeen. I married a woman from Ireland with one daughter. That marriage was a disaster —lasted for seven months and had it annulled. I joined the air force at nineteen. That was a disaster. I got out on medical four and a half months later. My life for the first, I say, thirty years was a complete disaster. I never could do anything right. Everything was all screwed up.

Then one day I woke up and I said to myself, "It's time to make a new beginning." I went to California and I started cooking. I been a cook for something like over thirty years. I travel a lot, I do. I used to do a lot of amphetamines. I lived on it for over twenty years. I had another wife, which nobody knew about. That marriage lasted for about four and a half years and then I had to make a decision—do I give up the wife or do I give up the amphetamines? 'Cause she couldn't take it. 'Cause I could stay up three or four days, sleep four or five hours, and get up, 'cause I had two jobs. We had everything we wanted except she had no love. So we got a divorce. I married the amphetamines.

I got two heart attacks. I wound up with last rites in 1974 at Metropolitan Hospital — an overdose on coke and amphetamines. The doctor told me then to stop, and I said no. I mean there's no way I'm gonna stop. So I continued, and I had a second heart attack in 1978, and I was in Roosevelt Hospital for two and a half months, and the doctors told me if you stay high and you get high, you gonna die.

That sort of made a little rude awakening. I stayed straight off of the amphetamines cold for a while, but due to the amount of traveling—I'm a very free–spirited kind of person. If that means getting up, quitting a job in the middle of the night, I'll do it. I been across the United States eleven times, been to Europe four times, traveled from California, from San Diego…stopped at every town. I worked. I love to travel.

I came back. I took a job at a hospital. I was at the hospital for nine and a half years. I had it made. Coke and amphetamines started coming back to me because I had an unlimited supply. I had all the doctors giving them to me because I would bring them down to the pharmaceutical every morning and seal them off—amphetamines. For the last two years of the job people couldn't tolerate me. I was trying to rush everything even though I was in charge—I wouldn't give them any slack. I didn't think it showed. Then one day I walked into my supervisor's office and I said, "I quit." I had a beautiful apartment—27 West 65th Street, Manhattan—paid nine hundred dollars rent. And I gave up everything, gave up everything that I had. And I moved into a place called the Amtrak Tunnel.

It hasn't been easy living in the tunnel. You have to go out for wood everyday. You have to go out for water everyday. You have to go out for food everyday. You have to make sure nobody bothers your area—your space—everyday.

Bernard was a good cook. We could have tunnel stew, which means everything went in the pot that wasn't glued down. Our best one was home fries with franks—we get hotdog rolls. We ate a lot of potatoes—home fries, 'cause they was cheap; ninety–nine cents for five pounds. Eggs and potatoes. I got him into my knockwurst. Now he's in love with Hillshire sausage. But either you got to buy the bottle of crack or Hillshire sausage, which one you gonna do? 'Cause they're both the same price. We've had some good times around that fire, but we've had some arguments. When he and I have an argument you can hear us from 91st to 99th. I mean I yell and he yelled. But I yell louder.

The last two years I been collecting cans. Sometimes cans can be embarrassing when people look at you, but I've never in two years or two and a half years or how long—I've never asked anybody for anything with a cup, never stood on a corner, never panhandled. As long as there was a can that I could see, I picked it up, I take it to the store. That's one thing that I can say for myself.

Roughly I would get up between five–thirty, six o'clock. I go out for my cans. I hit as many areas as I can. Generally I get through about eight o'clock. Then I deal with the stores. Now that's another whole other ball game. A lot of stores don't want to deal with cans in the morning. A lot of 'em say the machines are off and stuff like that.

There was a friend of ours down at 79th Street, and Bernard was going out with some cans and this guy says to Bernard, "You got to pay to go out." And Bernard looks at him—this guy by the name of Leon—and Bernard said to him, "Don't you know who I am? I'm the Lord of the Tunnel." So a couple of weeks later Bernard came up top and Leon was sitting there and he said, "Oh, by the way everybody, this is the Lord of the Tunnel." And that's how he got the name. Lord of the Tunnel.

The wood we got from dumpsters in the area—people throw out wood. Food we got from the schools or supermarkets or else bought it—depending on if we had money. Mainly I try to buy it. I don't like dealing with schools and what not. Buy what you need, take it down, and it's over with.

There were more than seven people at our place at one time. I would say from 125th down to 72d at one time there had to be forty people livin' all in different areas. All in their little spots they called theirs. Stay away from them, that's about it. I don't get along with a couple people down there—they think they're it and they're not. It's only an existence. Blink an eye and it's all gone.

I had people try and follow me when I was living down in the tunnel—maybe thought they were gonna mug me or whatnot. But once I got down on the tracks, I own the tracks 'cause I know the tracks. I could walk in the dark backwards if I had to 'cause I know every rock. That's where I lost him. 'Cause no one would ever follow me. I've had people try to mug me in the park—my first year out here before they knew who I was—so I carry a straight razor and I will cut you rather than even look at you. It's like, I won't try and hurt you if you don't try and hurt me. Do anything you want as [long as] it doesn't involve me. When it involves me, then I have something to say about it. Until then, I don't care what anybody does—unless it happens in the tunnel. When it happens in the tunnel, then it is my concern. But if it happens, like I say, up top or below 91st Street, then it was ok. It didn't matter to me.

You get to meet some weird people coming through the tunnel. We met young graffiti artists. In fact we met one of the best graffiti artists—his name was Freedom–Chris. He just did a mural down in our place. It must be something like sixty–foot by thirty–foot. Then we had a fellow by the name of Sane. He died recently—fell off a bridge. And he did a piece right on our wall about the mind, intellectuality, that man is screwing up the whole world. And it really looked nice.

Then we got a lot of kids come through—guys and girls—that try to hassle us. But most of them, most of the people down there, know us. The word among the kids spreads a lot. Bernard is dark skinned. I'm light skinned. Bernard is six–foot–three and I'm five–eleven, and so they more or less—they respect us. They had to test Bernard. Bernard's not the one you want to test, anyway. I have to give him credit for that. He doesn't back up, neither do I. And the kids more or less—like I said—they leave us alone.

For a while I was letting Bernard run my life. I didn't think there was anything but the tunnel. I didn't think I could exist up top. I had let some thirty–five–, thirty–six–year–old run a fifty–year–old man's life. Today I'm trying to get it back. It's kinda hard. It's kinda scary 'cause down there I had security. I didn't have to pay rent. I had what I needed.

A lot of times I'd sit on the tracks and do a lot of thinking. Most of my thinking was done at night when everything is quiet, everything is dark. The tunnel is nice in the light. You see the graffiti on the walls, you hear the train go by. But at nighttime, when everything is silent, is when you can really find yourself.

The tunnel's not bad. The tunnel's a good place if you want to find out who you are. But when you do find out who you are, you have to move out or the tunnel will eat you up like it ate me up for several years. Like I say, I built everything up around the tunnel. Now I have to learn to build it around myself.

Manny

I was sitting in the park one time—always after work I used to come and sit and have beers. When, seeing Bernard so many times, I offered him a beer. And that's how I met him. And he invited me to his place, and ever since then it's just been history—been a good friend. And I had a few problems about myself, too. And it's the only place I really like to go. I really trust Bernard. He's always there when you need him.

I used to work at M & S Contracting and a few real estate companies in the Bronx and Manhattan. Been unemployed ever since—out of work for about a year. So I'm on public assistance right now. I'm living down in the tunnel with Bernard. For how long, I don't know—no plans. I feel comfortable there. Too much problems at home. My mother passed away two years ago. A week after my mother was dead, my father brought in a new lady. She practices a lot of witchcraft. She throws a lot of powders on my clothing—candles, crosses backwards—and I'm spooked about that because I come from a Spanish background. In Puerto Rico they practice that on some parts of the island—Santería. Very evil stuff—they can spike your food or drink, a picture, or an article of clothing, whatever. And it does work. My mother was killed with Santería.

And things that she has done to me in the past. She's actually my father's brother's ex–wife, and he has dented the family so hard. My sisters doesn't talk to him anymore. Half of the family doesn't talk to him anymore. It's just been chaos for the past two years.

[My father] used to beat up on his parents. He came from an alcoholic family. Sometimes the son doesn't have to be an alcoholic but he can pass it on to his family. And his brother was an alcoholic. It was a very dysfunctional family. All those beatings and verbal abuse that he used to give me and my mother has caught up with me because, you know, it's been hurting me so much. Sometimes I can't think straight. I hold back a very lot of pain. I don't really trust nobody. Bernard's been the only friend I got. He's the only person I trust. He knows I don't trust everybody. I'm hurt inside. I'm suffering. But bear the time, I hope it heals away.

So, I prefer to be in the streets. Bernard lets me in the tunnel. And just survive, a day at a time, than to be in that type of surrounding. I was born and raised out of that apartment, and my father takes her side instead of his own children. And I keep no contact with my sisters. If I ran up to 'em right now and tell 'em I'm in the street, which they know, and they would not give me a hand. So I just don't bother with it. I stay by myself.

One time I was coming from the store to Bernard's place in the tunnel, and about three or four guys started following me. And they started saying, "Let's smoke that white boy," referring to me. So I got pretty scared because it was about two o'clock in the morning. So I said to myself, "Well, I know where I'm going. I don't know about them." So I went into the steps of the tunnel, and one guy came halfway down the steps and told his friends to forget about it, that they didn't know who was I with, or if I had a gun or a weapon, that they wouldn't go down there.

I feel safe in the tunnel because I don't care how big you are—even if you have a gun or a weapon—if you don't know where you're going or if you never been in there—it has no light, no types of light. You're in big trouble. You wouldn't go in no matter what you got in your hand because you don't know where you're walking into. You know it's so dark that you can't even see your own hand in there at night.

Larry

I been a friend of Bernard's for approximately ten years. I came here about 1986.
It was cold like it is right at this point. We sort of stumbled on one another.
I, unfortunately, became homeless and I was looking for somewhere that I could
just rest my head. It was a fluke that I ran into Bernard. I was walking down the
river, and I saw the gate was open—that was before they had the repair of the
gates—and my curiosity got the best of me, and I just sort of wandered down
here. Bernard was going to get some water. I asked him for a cigarette, and so we
just struck up a conversation. We started talking, and we had a lot of things in
common. He had a stretch of vacant rooms, and he offered me one.

I immediately jumped at the chance to take one of them because I was just out here
in the cold, and I had been going from place to place. I had lived in the public
shelters, which are very treacherous to live in, and I just couldn't stay there. And
I said, "Rather than be in those shelters, I would just try my luck in the streets."
I don't have any family here in New York that I could of went to for assistance, so
I was just alone and just searching. This has been my home—I can say "home"
in quotes—for approximately five years out of the nine or ten that I have been
roaming the streets. Sometimes I would try to find a place through one of the
public agencies, but that just hasn't come through. And so I find myself again
doing the circle—coming back to base one. Hopefully I'll be here for a while and
then probably gather some funds and try to find a place that I can call my own.
At this point I don't know how long that will be.

The shelters was horrendous. There was not too much supervision because of the volume of people. They tried to organize things but things were always out of hand with so many people, and there wasn't enough staff there to really supervise the clients. I was there for about a year —[fights] constantly —enough to bring the ambulance there on the average at least about four times a week to take somebody out on a stretcher or a wheelchair. Guys beaten, just beaten with sticks, broom handles, whatever they had in their hand to beat 'em with. There were only about twenty–five security guards there to keep control of twelve hundred men. Sometimes [the guards] would push them and occasionally they would hit them. For just —well, there's so many things the clients would do —theft, for pushing someone, or just start arguments, that type of thing.

There was a lot of turmoil and there was a lot of inconsistency there. They would just feed on whatever was the urge for them to feed on. I just couldn't stay there, so I severed my ties with the shelter system.

I wouldn't want to build a shanty because it's too volatile. You never know what's going to happen there in the structure. This is a solid structure. And there's not a lot of traffic here like you find up above this. On the streets there's too much traffic and there's too many things that can endanger your life. It's sort of difficult for a person to just wander in because of the locks on the gates. They would really have to want to come here because there's only two exits —72d Street and 123d Street.

I look into dumpsters, and sometimes I go to the churches or places where they'd be handing out pantry food. There's a hodgepodge of things that's usually thrown out — just anything that the grocery store or restaurant determines they don't need. For example, a grocery store might have day–old bread that people wouldn't accept, so they'll throw that out —so I have bread. They might throw eggs out that were damaged, milk that's been sitting too long. It's still edible. For example, I would go to Sloan's because they usually put food out around eight o'clock. Food Emporium —they put it out at ten o'clock in the dumpsters or in bags. I usually untie the bags, look to find out what the contents is. And then after I have examined it and found what I want, I tie the bags back neatly.

Some of the other places I go to is the churches. Like I go there on Wednesday to a church on 93d Street. They usually have pantry at that time. They give a single man a bag of groceries which contained pasta, breads, some canned goods. One or two might contain meat, tea, and maybe some cheese or something or some fruit. I go to several of those during the week. Riverside Drive Church—I go there. They give about once a month. And I usually go to two soup kitchens because you can eat there. Like on 114th Street and Broadway—there's a church there. Mondays, Wednesdays, and Fridays—you have to get a ticket in advance. They have two servings, one at twelve and at one o'clock, and you eat there. You can eat in and then they give you things to take with you—if they have anything left over. And I bring that back to the tunnel and I share it.

I have fleeting thoughts [of returning to Cleveland], but I've come this far so I'm just going to bear it out. I've made several visits over the last ten years—visiting family. They're aware that I'm in the shelters. They want me to come there, but I feel as though I would be cheating myself for wanting to be here in New York. And I guess this is part of the New York experience—on this level. There is a lot of diversity here and this is part of it, this scene that I'm in right now. And there's a lot of opportunity here, and you just have to be there at the right time at the right place. Unfortunately, I haven't been able to be there at the right time or the right place.

Alcoves and ledges

Burtram

I used to pull burglar jobs. But it doesn't mean [stealing] cans. There's no real need to get in trouble again, 'cause every time you turn around there's another car window in the way, see? I was in jail for pulling burglary jobs. And twice, three times, they gave me two bullets and Rikers Island. And then they gave me a strict sentence — two to four. They told me that if I come back again that I'm a three–time loser and that I'm gonna get fifteen to twenty–five — life. So I found some kind of way to dismiss the subject and change my act — doing such a thing by myself. And I just showed up. Bernard saw me walking by one day. I came over here accidently on purpose. I didn't realize that this is the place. And he talked to me and I was told — I was walking down there — that I was gonna live down there.

[My father] was Puerto Rican. He was part Japanese. I'm half Japanese and half Negro. I was born in King's County Hospital. My mother's name is Barberton. My other mother's name — one I was living with — is Bernice Lee. See, I was a bastard when I was a little boy. Her husband's name is David Lee. He had sex with my real mother, and that's how they have me.

There was five of us. My mother was separated. We was living on welfare after that. That's the whole story about my other mother. She got a civil service job — typing and all. Got in trouble too — something that I did. And she reported it to the police station. That wasn't the first instance. The first instance I had a twenty–two — a little pistol, had these little bullets in it — but I hid it in my room. Just sounded like my mother tripped on it accidently on purpose as she was looking through one of the drawers. They found it and reported it. That's where the fear was, "Was I gonna really kill somebody with the gun?" But before that happened I fired it to make a fool out of them.

[We lived at] 62d Street and Amsterdam Avenue [and] on Tenth Avenue. I went to St. Paul's. I got into a fight a couple times, couldn't calm down and socially adjust.

So I had to scam—fear and anger—right away. Anyway, after I had these fights, these sex problems set in, and that's how I always used to get in trouble with the police. But there wasn't no vicious sex problems. The reason was because I wasn't really living with my real mother. It was just being secluded without really feeling free to talk to anybody at all at a time like that. That's how it happened to me.

I went down south for a while when I was on welfare. I used to live on 94th Street— one of those welfare hotels—when I was on welfare. And I was just looking for that knowledge, so I pocketed the money and went down south. And soon I caught up on them with the pool game and went to the carnival. I read all these books. Went to the carnival and played with that weapon. First I did it at Coney Island and I won it—the Elvis Presley prize.

And every other day I used to walk down there to the Bowery—real early in the morning. Sometimes used to find all this money laying around the cars—all coin hunting. It's unbelievable about my pockets. Pockets was funny. Sometimes when I used to walk back here they used to be bulgy with all this change. And then I started bringing food back, when they had extra food. After a while I got over it, started calming down. But I was drinking wine.

These church people stop me and ask me would I like to come up and listen to services, and they eat up there, and they have beds too. They stop me and try to show me that—like a brother, not like a hit–and–run story–person that will just run over somebody. I got to keep my distance from people like that.

I don't believe in getting on welfare. [I collect] cans, bottles, plastics—twenty, thirty dollars when they put those blue bags out. I basically take care of the neighborhood. I mean there's plenty of guys around but what I had to do—I had to come up with some fancier ways of doing it because I didn't have a pushcart. You need a pushcart —two of them.

I used to live in practically all them watchtowers where the train comes and goes out in the clearing down there at the end. When I first started out I was living at the end watchtower. When I was with Cookie Puss, I was living at the first one beyond my place, and I used to always go out there with her. Cookie Puss was a gal I met when I was in France. Cookie is "Italian" now. Some C.O. shot her in the head with a .38—down here. We used to always go get cans and things like that, but James Bond…

No, I don't have the possession of a gun. All I have to do is trust the blow to get James Bond. He was just walking around and I noticed him. I put my stuff down. He walked up on me, and I actually punched his motherfucking headlights off. One other time, James Bond was in the neighborhood and right by the Arab store. He was walking across the street. I walked up to him and actually crashed his face in. I could believe in my blow.

Sometimes when you're walking down the street and you hear somebody talking, might not pertain to you or anybody else. But the understanding of that is "kill." Sometimes I just don't feel right walking on the sidewalks with all that noise that they be making. And then I just try to pave my own way, get out of the street, relax my feet. And that's when I usually find money laying around them cars— just like that. Figure that out.

Ria

I've only been living down here [in the tunnel] since the end of the summer. I've been on the streets for about three years. A guy brought me down here to get high with him and afterwards, we sat over there on the staircase. And I looked over and I seen the hole in the wall and I stuck my head in and that's how I started staying in there. There was clothes and stuff there but no one was living there. It just looked good. It looked comfortable. It looked safe. I was indoors, away from the environment out here. You know, this is like a real nice place. I could set up a home in it instead of sleeping on the benches up on Broadway. I was up there for a couple of years maybe. I'd sleep on a bench, on the grate, in the subway, whatever.

I was born on 103d and First Avenue but I was raised in Connecticut [after] about three or four [years of age]. Waterbury [high school]. I went to college at Stone [School of Business] in Hamden for a year. I took up word processing. Then I came out here to see the fast lights and all that good stuff. And well, it didn't turn out so great for me.

I worked in Staten Island, Miller's Pharmacy. I was there for about five years. After that I got involved in crack, alcohol. My life was not too good. Curiosity, just curious. I wanted to know what made people go out of their way to get this little thing in a plastic vial. I wanted to know why they would be there for three minutes and then they'd get up and run to get another three hours at it. I wanted to know what made them do that. [Friends] were smoking it and I tried it. I liked it, too. Now I know why they do it.

In a way I am [addicted] but when I came out here, I ended up doing good. I had a job. I got on welfare and then I had another part–time job. I worked in the municipal building as a receptionist. Then I had a weekend job, Stapleton Guard, armed guard dogs, something to that effect. Some Staten Island place. I was working as a guard. So I had three jobs. I was doing good. I worked all the jobs at one time. Limelighting, getting everything I wanted. I had money galore.

And right now what I'm going through, I'm having fun. I'm still learning what goes on in the city. I mean, I haven't been out here five or six years like some other people have been. But I'm still learning how people are surviving out here. It's a different world from the way I was living before. I was living in the limelight. I gets my three dollars without even blinkin' an eye. Now I don't even know where my first penny's going to come from. At this magnitude, didn't matter if I was drinking or not.

I think [it has been] about five or six [years since the job ended]. I lost count. Been on welfare, public assistance. I went on there and I really didn't need it. I just got on because this girl showed me how to get on it, so it was really like a fraud. Then afterwards when they wanted me to go for every six months recall interview, I never showed up so they cut me off. Now I guess I'm too lazy to go, so I survive through the streets.

I'd pick up cans. And other than that, I find stuff in the garbage cans and I sell it. Find an old piece of cloth, lay it on the street, put its junk there and just sell it. I made up to ninety dollars in one day. There's other people that have been doing it for a while who've made hundreds. And they come out good because they go down into the Village and they find really nice stuff. I look around up here 'cause I don't like hopping the train. I'm not gonna pay a dollar and a quarter to go downtown 'cause I don't have it. I'd rather take that dollar and a quarter and buy me something to eat.

I feel free. No bills. Nobody knocking on the door. You get a head in the window every once in a while. That's it. Other than that, happy–go–lucky. You get your weirdos. You get people that walk up to you and proposition you and you get your people who try to take advantage of you. Several occasions I almost gotten raped. But I carry a weapon. I carry an icepick. Punctured a lung. Now he sees me and he goes to the next block. It's a little bit more dangerous than for a man. You have more risks. You have the risk of getting raped, mugged more easier than a man. I've stayed in little corners and stuff by myself. Like I said, I have my own protection. I protect myself very well.

I am [still on drugs]. My body don't run on it. Like I said, I was curious. Now I'm getting sick of it. I'm getting ready to return back to civilization shortly. Yes I am. I'm ready to move into an apartment. It's gonna be kind of rough though because I've gotten so used to living in the streets. You know, instead of me finding wood to make a fire, I'll just have to turn a knob. And it's gonna take a little while.

I got to get out of here. It's like living in the jungle. It's wild. I mean, I came down to this park and seen things that would make an average man quiver. I mean I've seen a girl over here actually get raped, and I didn't hear her screaming so I figured that's what she wanted to do. I didn't know he had her tied up. You know, girl down here got pushed off the wall, from right there where you see, up at the top. She got hospitalized, that was about it. She didn't die though. Right now there's three of us [on the ledge]. But there's other people down further and there's other people up this way. I've fell off the ledge a couple of times but, you see all that stuff that's down there, if it wasn't for that I would have been hurt.

Altogether I have four [children]. They're in Connecticut with my mother. [Their father] was my first boyfriend. He just departed.

I'm thirty. That's about it. That's all of me.

Marcos

I was two years old [when the family arrived from Cuba]. We lived here. My mother worked in the garment district for twenty–five years as a seamstress. [My father] worked at importing products, and then they got divorced and he went over to Puerto Rico. My grandmother was into voodoo—a priestess. My grandfather was a Mason. I was raised the opposite—strict Catholic—because my mother was afraid of that stuff. I lived with a priest and the nuns when I was a kid, and they wanted me to be a priest. So the whole thing was, I'm not imagining that people are evil.

I studied anthropology at Columbia because my dad always wanted me to. It was beautiful before they got divorced. They divorced early, when I was five years old. He always said, "Listen, I can't stay with you all the time, but keep learning all the time." So he used to always take us to the Museum of Natural History. So I kept on studying, I kept that interest.

I don't like to give too much of my private ancient history. That was so long ago— about twenty years ago—they threw me in there. I was thrown in. Once about six weeks, and then another time five weeks, and then another time nine days, and that was it. I'm not a danger to anybody—it was to myself—it wasn't to anyone else. I wasn't attacking anyone else. I didn't go out and start murdering people, killing people, cutting people up. What I tried to do was kill myself, actually.

One of the times I tried to set myself on fire was to protest the war —the Vietnam War —like Buddhist monks did. I was also into Buddhism at the time, so I was protesting my own way. I set myself on fire, which was kind of radical, but the strange thing was I didn't feel any pain. I was meditating, and I didn't feel any pain at all. Eighty–ninth Street, right on the street, just off Broadway—I was just doing it on my own. I wasn't doing it in front of any television cameras or anything like that. Then they put me in the nut hospital for that reason.

In those days I was doing drugs, I admit it now. I was smoking a lot, and I was doing acid and all that stuff. People were messing with my mind —psychically harassing me. And they still do that. Their minds were harassing me. And I was never used to hearing people because I was raised Christian. I thought it was God, and it was really people —demonic—just messing with my mind. But when you're on LSD your mind gets to a higher consciousness, so you hear more things.

Twenty years ago they gave me Thorazine, and I had side effects. They gave me half the lethal dose for six weeks and then five weeks and then nine days, and I got Bell's palsy and tarsal dyskinesia, kind of facial neurological paralysis. My eyes wouldn't close. Side of my lips wouldn't close. The side of my face looked like Quasimodo.

That's why they put me on Social Security, because they had put me in a nuthouse a few times. And I spoke with one of the psychologist guys and guess what? He goes, "What do you believe about God?" I said, "Well, I believe God helps me. I was raised Catholic, and I believe in Divine Providence, and if you're good, God will really help you if you need." And I feel that in a way the garbage is almost like the Holy Grail. Sometimes when I have no food, I find food in the garbage can, and books and clothes that have helped me.

[My best friend] O.D.'d in 1980 on cocaine. He used to be a bartender at a club. It was just off Fifth Avenue and 38th Street. I knew him for many years. His father and his grandmother were good friends of mine. That kind of traumatized me, and I had a nervous breakdown. I never realized that you can go almost crazy from sorrow, because he was my brother. Not family brother like blood, but they like adopted me, and I lived with them for years. He died in my hands and I tried—I called EMS— they did not come. Police came and tried to ransack the place for drugs, and there were no drugs there. I said, "Why don't you help him?" I had massaged his heart and given him mouth–to–mouth resuscitation, and they could have put refibulators on him and have saved him. They didn't even try.

And when he died, it really was a shock. I was just wandering around the streets for years. And a girl I used to live with—if it wasn't for her, I probably never would have come back from madness land. I wasn't evil or nothing. I never hurt nobody or nothing. It's just everything's so different.

I went and I found a place down there—Liberty Park, now. There was a landfill down there. I lived down there for years, and then all of a sudden I left and came uptown.

I just kept living on the street, and I lived with my mom and Ariadne. I lived with her for three years. We had our own place for a while, and then that fell through and she came to live with my mom and me for another two years. Ariadne was French. She was the first one that got me into the flute. She played flute and piano. Her mother and father are both world–renowned musicians. She used to go to Hunter College. She wanted to be with me so much she just left school. I told her stay in school, keep working.

I more or less believe it was crazy love. But she was very jealous. That was one of the reasons I broke up with her. If I even looked at another girl she would hit me. She got very volatile. She had problems sometimes. She would stab herself sometimes, thinking I didn't love her. She was my love. She was so beautiful. She died, though. After we broke up she met this other guy. He was fucked up. He was a junky kid. He was the son of these rich people, and she died in a year from being with him. I mean he didn't kill her, but it was negative influence because he got her into heroin.

I lived on the streets ever since then. I came down here. I been down here eight years, ever since I broke up with her. I knew about the tunnel for years, even before. I would come here and visit the place and check out the graffiti when I was just a teenager. I'm forty–one now.

I don't ascribe any mystical thing to [living underground]. It's just free. Not about a monetary free thing—but I feel free here. I'm not constricted by people crowding me like over there where everybody's in a matchbox. You could hear through the wall. Where's your privacy? Over here there's privacy and spaciousness. I feel comfortable, and this is my home. I like the artwork—it feels like I'm living in an art museum.

And people here, I know them as friends. People here respect each other's territorial integrity, and they know that everybody has their own. People always make a lot more problems all squelched in like sardines.

They started saying "the mole people." I started saying we should just call this the freedom tunnel.

Toward the south end

John

I was born in Brooklyn, '42. My father died when I was five. I was raised in a home 'cause my mother couldn't take care of me, my brother, and my two sisters. We all was put in different places. I ran away from the institution, and I been on my own since I was sixteen. Me and Mother never really got along. I had my own place here in New York. I used to go down to see her once a week, brought the groceries to her and a carton of cigarettes. But that wasn't enough. I fell asleep there one day, and if it wasn't for my grandmother, I wouldn't be here today. My mother woke me up with a butcher's knife to my throat 'cause she wanted money to go out 'cause she was [drinking gesture].

I didn't have no place to stay, and I wasn't gonna ask nobody. So that's how I started sleeping in the subway stations. On the trains you just go from one end of the station to the next. "And this," I said, "I got to stop." I used to sleep on the park benches. Then I figured I better find a little bit of a safer place to sleep. 'Cause when I used to sleep out here, some nights in the park, kids come by. They threw a bottle at me once. It caught me in the head. I had my hand there, but… First I slept by the handball court before you got down to the tracks. Then I said, "Well look, let me go and walk through the tunnel here, see what I could find."

So I kept walking to the back and found this house and started to clean it and fix it up. They were there for the workers. My place, I think, was the kitchen because I found a refrigerator in there and a room for supplies and stuff like that. This was long before the pier burned down, way before that, about seventeen or eighteen years, or something.

I had to walk around the street at night to look for things that I want to put into it. And sometimes I had to carry it ten to fifteen blocks just to get it down. All that stuff I carried from the streets down into there myself. If it looked good, I would take it. I decided that if I want to stay here, let me make it look like a home.

Then I start finding animals and bringing animals down there—finding them in the street. And I said to myself, "I had animals around me to take care of, keep me above water." In other words, you gave me a swift kick in the ass, like, "Look, I need food to eat and stuff like that." And that's what kept me going. That's why I had all these animals. 'Course they got pregnant. I guess I got about fifteen, twenty cats, something like that—twenty–five—plus I had two or three dogs. I didn't have the cats to keep out the rats. I had [gotten rid of] the rats before I had those cats in there. I got rid of everything. I had the whole place cleaned, sterilized, and everything else. If you keep your place clean, and you don't have garbage laying around, you're not gonna have no rats.

My routine was in the afternoons—I'd say around lunchtime—I would go up towards the school on 77th Street, get some food—get chicken, sandwiches, milk, juice, whatever. They come out with bags and stuff, and I take what I need—left over from the same day, not the day before. I take that stuff that they don't use. Sometimes they come out with four or five bags full. You see the trays here? This is how the school food comes. And I used to get sometimes twenty trays, given to me from the custodians and stuff. Let's say maybe fish, maybe meat loaf, whatever. And that's what I fed my animals with.

Never had to ask nobody for nothing. That's how come I never used to get along with nobody in the tunnel, even when I used to feed everybody down there. And I could give them extra food, and I still have extra. I always keep food. I look at it this way. At least you could offer me something. I may say no, but at least once in a while offer. 'Cause I give. I give more than what somebody would offer me.

I'd do my food shopping and I'd come back, put everything away, and cook what I'm gonna cook up. And what's left I leave in the pot, put it up on top of the cabinet there, cover it up, and I leave it there for the next feeding, and I eat some of it myself, and I take a nap. And I may get up one, two o'clock in the morning. I may get up earlier than that if I wake up. And I go out and I look around the streets and see what I could use around the house.

I washed dishes, I worked for the Central Park Zoo, worked for the Ringling Brothers with the circus. I did all sorts of jobs just to get by. Over school I knew the principals, teachers—wash their cars, make money that way. I never stood on the corner asking people for nothing. Sometime I sweep up down the hallway, make about ten or fifteen dollars that way. But I worked for my money. I was doing odds and ends. And if maybe I don't got nothing to do, I'm down there working on taking care of my place. But I spend a lot more time in my place than I spend out here in the street. I could relax in my house more than I could in the street.

It's nice and quiet, except for the cars overhead. But it's also dangerous, too. A lot of people will tell you it's not dangerous. That's a lot of nonsense. It is 'cause you don't know who's walking on the tracks. I've walked those tracks two or three o'clock in the morning by myself, just coming in. Maybe I'm carrying something in or maybe I'm just coming out. And I'm walking from my house to 72d Street, no flashlight or nothing. And I generally can see if somebody is coming, I guess because you get use to the dark. But I just go out, get my food for my animals, come back in, lock up while I'm in the house.

I was attacked twice. The first time I was attacked—these poles that say "No Parking" on them, I got beat up with one of those. I was on my way to my house, had all my ribs fractured. Second time, people I was living back there with—I was giving them food and what not. One day I come in and they was all settin' me up. And I had to get my nose operated on. I got a wire back here. This is all plastic back here, and from the same people I tried to help. They walked past me, so I asked this one person for a light because I didn't have a match. Soon as I lit my cigarette I got hit right in the temple. I went down and somebody said, "He went down like a sissy." I was out of it. And so I went in my house and—I was bold—you know, you come out with a knife, a gun, whatever. I stood, I tried to eat a little something but I couldn't, 'cause I could feel all my bones cracked. So around two or three o'clock in the morning I got up and I went to the hospital. Stayed in the hospital for about two or three weeks. When I came back from the hospital they disappeared. They knew I was coming back down. They was out of there.

See, they all thought I was one of these so–called punks, until one day I showed everybody. And I almost put somebody in the hospital once, damn near killed 'em in front of everybody down there. So that's how I got everybody straight. That was it. They left me alone. Let's say, I had more than what they had. I guess they got jealous or they wanted what I had, I don't know. It was the people that you knew, those the ones that stole from you, not strangers.

A lot of things happen in the tunnel—you get fights down there. But I never was bothered, really, until I started decorating my house. People didn't like the idea because I was outdoing everybody, and I was supposed to be a big shot and this and that. Donnie and Rick—I'm the one that told 'em that they could move in that house there. I gave them that house. Joe—the house that Joe's living in—I put Joe into that house. Anybody living in those houses, I put 'em in those houses. See, I could have all those houses for myself. That's why I had a different type of a house, 'cause I was the first one there.

Joe

I was born here in Manhattan, Yorkville—East Side. I had an apartment, but I was having bad flashbacks and I had to get out—flashbacks from Vietnam. Still have them but not as bad. Firefights that I was in, places getting overrun, stuff like that. I was in the North. Four tours—'64, '65, '67, and '68. I was Special Forces. My job in Vietnam was to go in and retrieve downed pilots or to give the enemy a hard time. I enlisted—had a court order. I punched some diplomat in the face one night. He gave me the finger when I asked him for the time, so I punched him out. I had a court order to join—join or go to jail. So I went in the army, and it was just like going to jail.

I was in Camp Eagle and some other places I can't talk about because we're still restricted. I can't talk about it because I signed a contract with the Special Forces. But I was all over. I did a lot of walking. I didn't ride too much. I was hit four times, wounded four times, got four purple hearts. [The Veterans Administration] gave me money. They gave me a hard time, though. They gave me 10 percent. I wound up with 100 percent.

I was married. I lost my wife and my kids. I had a kid that my money went to pay for the hospital and stuff. And I still haven't refiled since she died. And so I make out here—books, cans, whatever. She died from the infection Agent Orange, from me being over there. I had a child when I came back from 'Nam each time. The first time they hit 'Nam with Agent Orange it looked like it was snowing. Came down—it was like snow for three, four months at a time. Trying to kill the fields and everything. They said in later years that they didn't use it that early, but they were using it. They actually didn't use Agent Orange until 1968, I mean really use it. But they were testing it, using it around.

[After Vietnam] I got divorced. Everything ended. When the kid died and the other kid got sick, I got blamed for everything, so that was it. It was over. She died in 1971. And then the other kid got sick. And I was blamed for that because of the effects of Agent Orange. One had cystic fibrosis and they attributed it to the effects. They just found traces in the blood. The second oldest died in '73. It really got bad. You couldn't even look at the kid after while. One had asthma. And she had emphysema on top of that. Everything went. The immune system was shot. She looked like she was dying of AIDS. She wasted away to garbage. And they were all beautiful–looking kids. When they all died, I just threw out their pictures and that's it. I had five daughters. I had two sets of twins, and I had one that didn't make it at all, so it doesn't matter. I only have one that's alive now. Her name is Patricia, and she's somewhere, I don't know. I haven't talked to her.

I got emphysema but not that bad. It's bad certain days — if it gets too smoky down here, if it gets too smoky anywhere. If I go by the buses, I can almost pass out. Besides, I got the pills. I go to the V.A., they say, "Hello, good–bye," and that's it. I haven't collected [disability benefits] since my daughter died. It takes me a year to get them, and then they screw you around. I don't pay attention to [my wife]. I see her, I walk right past her.

In '72, I was walking around in the neighborhood, looking. Being in Special Forces, I found places where nobody else would ever go or want to go. And that's where I would go because nobody else would be there. And it would be nice and quiet. In '73, I lived in the front. It's not there anymore. It's where the scale used to be, where they used to weigh the trains. It was nice under there. I was here when Conrail was here, and the workers, the security guys walking up and down, thought at the time I was one of them because I just walked back and forth same like they did. Most of the time they ran the trains on that side, the coal trains, that was all.

I got up here about 1979. We took the gate off, and we could get out that way and it was easier. Plus when they took up all the tracks, it was easier to bring the wagons up. When you drag three hundred pounds of stuff on gravel it hurts you after a while. I'm not getting any younger, either.

I don't get welfare. Whatever I get out on the street is mine. Nobody's going to say nothing. Nobody's giving me nothing. I may be one of the few that are doing it. I stay here. I go to work every day. Sunday, I take a day off, go listen to the football game, watch TV. I'm on the street making money, collecting the cans. Doing the magazines and books. I don't ask nobody nothing. I don't beg. I know people out here in the neighborhood, they always say, "You need anything?" I always say, "I'm okay." If I don't make it today, I'll make it tomorrow or the next day. I mean everybody eats — cats and dogs, everybody.

I met [Cathy] through her mother, sitting in the park. The lady was in a wheelchair. I always used to say hello to her, kid around with her, ask her if she needed anything. She always asked if I needed anything. We'd kid around back and forth. And then one day she showed up. I thought she was the nurse, not the daughter. Really, I did. And I don't know, we just got together. She told her mother she was coming to see me. She came down, she never left. Her mother was still alive, too. And she said, "Go ahead, have a ball." That's the only time I put the doors on the room. There were no doors on here. Nobody came in here. Nobody bothered me. They came here, they were gonna have a problem.

[Cathy's] known me seven years. We're married—actually got married. She had one [child] before. She was married before. She was married to a Vietnam veteran, too—Spanish guy. He O.D.'d. He was a nice guy. He was a marine. He came from the Bronx. He was a tunnel rat [in Vietnam]. I know how it is to be a tunnel rat because I did that tour myself—flashlight and a gun, go down in the tunnels, visit people. If the enemy doesn't get you, "two step" will get you. That's a little snake. Take two steps and you drop dead. Pretty little white snake, bites you, you can say your prayers, you got it made. [Cathy's child] died, killed in [Central] Park—about two years old. Got hit in the baby carriage, right over by the castle—stray bullet. Eighty–four, I think. They're still looking for the guy. She went through a lot.

Cathy

[My mother] was there for me in her own way. She liked [Joe]. She worried about him, but you figure she had thirteen sons. I was the last child. I'm used to living around guys. It's going on eight years. [The first time] it was a little strange. It's not exactly living upstairs, but I found that it's not bad. It's not the greatest in the world, but when it's the only thing you have, it's what you have to do. [Joe] was a single male. He didn't exactly have women living with him. He had a bed and things like that. But he's a male and he was alone and it looked like a guy living anywhere — a slob. And then he just fixed it up better. We painted it, put in nice pillows and blankets and stuff like that — more color. He does the cooking. I clean, he cooks. No running water. That's it. Other than that, it's perfect.

I take medication for asthma and epilepsy. It doesn't matter where you live, what you're doing. If it comes, it comes. There's nothing you can do about it. I go out every day. I have friends. I go to the bar to see my friends and stuff like that. I don't hide. But everybody doesn't know everything about me either because it's none of their business. I don't ask them about them, and they don't ask about me. So, that's the way it is. Because some of them are my friends, they know where I live. But then there are others who are just acquaintances that I see when I see, and that's it. And they don't know nothing. They don't have to.

I don't want to bring any kids into this world. It's not worth it. It's not. There's too many kids out here now that aren't wanted, that are born drug–addicted. There's too many. I'm not going to bring a child into this. It's hard for me and Joe to manage now. We're gonna take care of a baby? What if I have a baby? They're gonna put me in a shelter. I'm not going to live in one of those places. That's why we're down here. So we don't have to live in those. Because they're dives. They're dumps. They're flea bags. That's exactly what they are. Because most the people that live in those shelters, they are mentally disturbed. They need care. And they're just tossed around and thrown around too. "So throw them in a corner somewhere. Oh, he'll die soon." I don't even want to talk about it anymore. It gets me mad.

I got my little family [eighteen cats], and that's enough. I don't need any more. They are all different, and if you're feeling bad they make you feel better. They're not like people, they're not two–faced. They don't have one side and then have another the next time. So that's why I love my animals. And they know they can depend on me.

I don't feel bad, because I know the other people. It's not the people down here, it's the people that come down here—then there's robberies and everything, and you know we can't complain to the Police Department. Fire. That's to me the worst I've ever been through down here—fire. Behind the building, and then when the houses burned down up there. The one guy, his lungs got burned. The other two, no, thank God. But that was the worst I've ever seen.

All [people "upstairs"] have to do is get up out of their warm bed and walk into the kitchen and make what they need. We got to get up and go in front of a fire and make sure you have your paper and your this and your that, or you don't eat. There's no delivery trucks coming down here with wood and supplies. We can't go to Macy's to get a down comforter for five hundred bucks. We got to find what we get. And if we're lucky enough to have a couple of dollars, we go and buy one for fifteen dollars or something. There's no easy thing down here. The garbage cans is where we find our stuff. They're putting locks on it because you got creeps out here that come around and throw the garbage all over. So the people who really need something can't get to it anymore. It makes it twice as hard on you now because at least you knew you had a couple of buildings you could go to and you knew you could find something that you could use. Now you can't go to these buildings no more. So now you've got to hunt and find another one.

You know, a lot of people have these ideas that we're living here because we want to live here. We don't live here because we want to. It's the only place we got. We're not wanted upstairs. You can't sleep on a park bench. You can't go anywhere. So this is what we got. People don't understand this. They think, "Oh God, they're all drunks and junkies and whatever." Yeah, there's a lot of them that do have a problem with alcohol and drugs. But most of the people that live down here, live here because this is all that they have. And they're just trying to make it the best way that they know how. And if at one time they have the chance to make it, they get the fuck out of here. But if they can't, this is all they got.

There's nobody coming down here—no politicians coming down here saying, "Oh, we'll give you an apartment. We'll do this for you, we'll do that for you." Nobody's coming down here. You don't see Giuliani and them running down here to help anybody. They're praying that, dear God, we have a bad winter and that we drop dead. I know what's going on here already with these people, so I don't even bother anymore. I make it the best way I know how. I don't steal. I don't panhandle. I just do what I have to do and that's it. That's it.

The south end

Ramón

Political problems. I was in jail for political problems. They prosecute me for a long time, and when I left Cuba they were looking for me to kill. That's why I escape. But you know, I came to the United States—I was afraid. 'Cause they say in the United States they discriminate, they're racist. That's true. There's racism in America, that a problem. But this is the best country in the world. No country like this. In Cuba, police see you on that corner more than fifteen minutes, "What the hell you doing? Let me see your wallet. Get the fuck out of here. You want a handcuff you motherfucker?" That what they say. When I left Cuba I was in third year for philosophy of history—to become a philosopher. Esteban came in 1980 like me. But the other one came about twenty years ago. You see, all we are Cuban.

The last four years I been homeless, that's the time I learn to love America, being homeless. You know why? Because you outside—the generosity. Nobody but the American people are that nice. Anybody give you some food. Anybody give you a dollar. Anybody help you. Everywhere you go you get food. You get clothes. You get a bed and a shelter—only in America. This is the best country. I love it. I told you, I cannot become a citizen here because I have problems—because of drugs. But I like here. I die here. Believe me, I don't care what I have to do, but I die here.

Uptown we have big, big record store. What happen is what happen to everybody who uses drugs—that's it. I don't blame nobody for my problems. It my fault, not society fault. You use drugs, that your problem. I went in jail for four months. [Rikers] was hard, man…homicide. I hate jail because jail in America it is hard, very hard. But when I came out, forget it, I lose everything. You in jail, you get trauma. Before I lose my store, I lose my apartment. I had two apartments. Then I went and rent room, and then I went to the street. Before come into the tunnel, I slept in the park.

This [tunnel] is not a life. We dead. The main problem with the homeless people— it's not missing a home, not missing food—the loneliness, that's the one. That's the main mental problem. You go outside there, everybody start watching me… It's incredible. You in the tunnel, everybody look at you down. You not a person 'cause you homeless.

Esteban

I've been [in the tunnel] about three years. I'd been down there sometimes and had visited Bernard. When I met Bernard, I was working over here by 90th Street. I had a job working as a private security [guard], but the job ended. Then everything ended. I met Ramón here also. I met him at my job, and ever since then we've been hanging out together.

I'm not a carpenter, but I know how to build a house. The rocks around the house are to prevent rats from coming inside. There's no light inside; the light comes at six in the afternoon when they turn on [the streetlamps in the park].

May 16, 1980 [I came to the United States]. My first four or five years, I was in Miami. From there they took us to a shelter in Texas. We were there for approximately a year. Some sponsors got us out of there and brought us to New York. Once here, we were with them for approximately one year. Then they took us to Welfare. They registered us there. We were free to do whatever we wanted. Then I started to meet people, older Cubans, who were here for many years. With them I learned to do many jobs. Almost all of them were construction workers, painters, and plumbers. I worked hard with them.

Then I left New York, and I went to New Jersey. There I got a job. I was working in a trailer factory. I was working there for approximately three to four years. Then they moved the factory, and once again we were left without a job. Then I tried again. I kept hanging in. I got another job painting—my thing has always been painting. I also painted at the trailer factory. I was the trailer painter. Then the other job I got was at a factory at Clinton, which is a chemical paint factory—mixing paint. I was there mixing paint and so on, but I think those paints had a very strong chemistry and they got to me and they gave me an allergy. That's where I ran out of luck. I couldn't work anymore.

From there I came back here to New York. And then I was hanging here and there—back and forth on the streets. But one day there was this guy who took my bag and with it all my documents. And because I have no money to get my documents again—that's why I haven't tried to get another job. Because without documents I can't do anything.

David

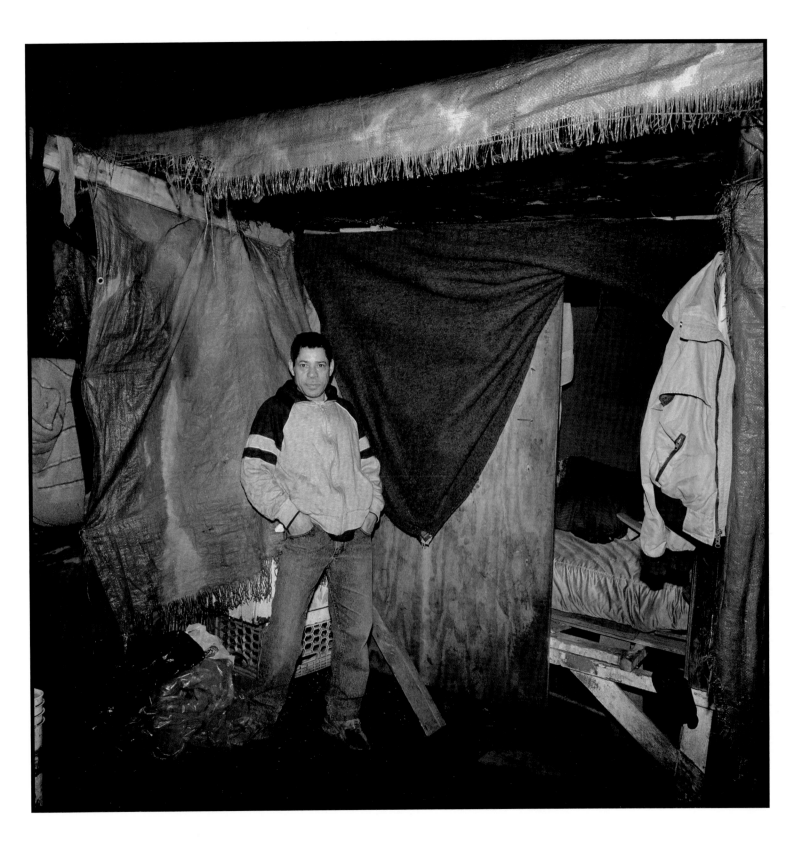

Five or six [years of age] I came over to the East Side [from Puerto Rico]. Then back in the fifties my family move from there to the Bronx, from the Bronx to Brooklyn, from Brooklyn to Manhattan. I lost [the apartment]. I can't afford to pay the rent. And I set it up down here. This place sometime a little spooky, sometime very cold, sometime the people don't get along. But it's a nice, quiet place.

I was over there [across the tracks] about a year and a half and then I came back, a year and a half. And when I came back, I move over here, back in '87. From there I spend most of six years around this tunnel, without coming out. I used to live here [adjacent dwelling] with a friend of mine but he went to California. So I don't want to live there alone—the place too big for a little guy. So I take over here and I move over here. For this I left my home.

I work now, temporarily, in a flower shop—six years. They don't pay me too much. They only pay about fifteen, twenty dollars. They don't pay very much because they—you're working off the book, you know.

[Before]—picking cans, making delivery, washing dishes, other jobs—temporary. I was on welfare once for a year, and then I quitted welfare. Was too much problem. Because sometimes you live down here, and you have to be there for the face–to–face come up. 'Cause sometime you miss it—they close up. Then you have to wait ninety days for to reopen it back up again. And so I stop for a year—been off welfare for a year, year and a half. I don't bother anymore.

I only sleep here. Nighttime I sleep. In the daytime I be running around in the flower shop or the OTB. With the OTB, I make delivery or play for the older peoples, play horses, or make delivery, or play somebody else's horses. That way I make money.

I don't keep food here. I go to restaurant and eat. You can keep food here, but anybody can walk in and walk out with your food, or your clothes, and everything—and you don't know who it is. Most of the people, young people—fifteen, sixteen, you know, eleven, ten—they like to burn. They like to destroy everything. A lot of problem.

Over there, anybody can walk in, drop a match, and go.

José

New York. Everybody said that. That's the dream. Everybody want to come over here.

About thirty–some years ago, I came to here from Puerto Rico. I was sixteen. My first job, I used to help cook in a restaurant, just to get the salad, things like that. Then I have to mop the floor. I make about fifty dollars a week. At that time it was good money, for my room only cost five dollars.

When I was working [for a] textile company, in the garment center, I was making twelve dollars an hour. I used to load trucks, unload them. But I had to break my back. They moved the factory to New Jersey, '75 or '80, so I lost my job. As soon as I lost my job, I didn't get no money to pay the rent.

I was married for over ten years. And then everything, it start getting — money —tight. She say, "Well. I'm leaving." And I say, "Well, good–bye. You leaving? Hey, you're free to go." She pack up and she leave.

I had a friend of mine that used to live over here, and he told me about [the tunnel]. And I know the whole story down here, so I build the house.

I can't complain. There's stuff, but you've got to do it. I get up around eight. I go pick up my paper. I come down here, read the paper for a little while. Then I go to sleep. In the afternoon I get up and cook. Then I start heating the water, and I take a shower. As soon as I take a shower, then I eat—go to sleep. See the whole thing is, when you live down here, you ain't got no life. So you got to do something—a couple of drinks, a lot of sleep. Like that, you don't get worried.

In the wintertime you hardly can take a shower, and I like to take a shower every day. I got the heater. I wait for the [street]light. [In the daytime] under the blanket [or] come outside and burn some wood. I read, any kind of magazine that I can get.

I go pick up my mail two times a week. Then when I got to go to the hospital, I go to the hospital to take care of my appointment. I got the high blood pressure. The heart is no good. They going to fix it up. They give me pills. They check my medicine. They check the blood pressure and take the blood out to test it.

I get a hundred dollars [welfare] every fifteen days. I go to A&P to look for the bargains. I don't look in the garbage. I'd rather use my little money that they give me to eat. I buy my stuff and bring it down here. And I cook myself—every night. I like to cook. I cook spaghetti, I cook rice. I do my salads. You learn over here. The only expense that I got is the cleaning, the food, that's it.

You don't leave no food around inside. Leave food, forget it. [The rats] going to go inside, no matter what. They dig a hole in the ground, all the way around. And it's a little dangerous, because sometime you sleeping, they bite. I was planning to put some wood, floor woods. Now they say that we have to move. Now I do nothing.

I was living very good. I had good apartment. Now I don't got nothing. Now look what I've got. I ain't got no other place to go. I ain't going to sleep in the street. I ain't going to shelter, that's for sure, because of what everybody says. They steal your money, they steal your clothes, you have to fight. You have to sleep with a bunch of those stinking… I'd rather be over here. Got my privacy. Got my water. I got my food, my TV, my heater, my blanket. Ain't no way in the world I'm going to go.

Epilogue

John left the tunnel in March 1991. Accompanied by his dog, Mama, he moved to upstate New York as a participant in a pilot program to train homeless individuals in organic farming.

Everybody had a bed to sleep in, I was the only one that didn't. I had the floor to sleep on. And I was the only one that didn't have a drawer or places to hang my clothes. I had to go sleep on the back porch. My Mama couldn't come into the house. I said, No, my Mama ain't gonna stay outside all night long.

In September 1991 John returned to the tunnel.

The day I came back, I must have got back around one, two o'clock in the morning. I was carrying two garbage bags full of stuff and my bayonet, my knife. I took that out of my bag and stuck it behind my back. I had Mama with me, of course. So I just came back down, went right into my house. The place was a mess. The only thing I did was clean up a spot on the bed where I could put Mama. I relaxed a bit, then I started cleaning up everything.

John left the tunnel again in late fall of 1992 to live with a friend in a nearby apartment building. He left his pets with tunnel residents. Mama died shortly after his departure and was buried in the tunnel. John completed correspondence courses in animal science and wildlife conservation and currently seeks employment in those fields. He walks dogs for area residents and finds part–time work painting and plastering.

I found what I was looking for.

Bob left the tunnel in the winter of 1994.

I woke up one morning and I had no food, no wood, no water. There was so much ice and snow outside you could barely walk. I just couldn't deal with it anymore.

Bob sought assistance at Peter's Place, a private service agency and currently has a room at a Brooklyn YMCA. He has undergone treatment for a heart condition.

Everything I've got now I've earned. I slept in chairs, I bused to churches for eleven months. The last seven months I've been at the Y. I've got my own linen, my own tv, my own clothes. It's something I can call my own. I don't want to lose that and start all over again.

Manny returned to his family's apartment in the neighborhood in 1994. He regularly visits Bernard in the tunnel.

Larry left the tunnel in 1994 for a men's shelter on the Lower East Side.

Ramón left the tunnel in the spring of 1995. He lives in a single–room–occupancy hotel in the neighborhood. He continues his friendship with Esteban but does not visit him in the tunnel.

Ria was forced to leave the tunnel when the arched grating through which she crawled every night was sealed up by park officials in the winter of 1995. She and her boyfriend found shelter in a stone arcade along the outside walls of the tunnel. She continued to live in Riverside Park after she gave birth to a baby girl at St. Luke's Hospital in the spring of 1995. Ria still sleeps in the park.

Bernard, Burtram, Marcos, Joe, Cathy, Esteban, David, and José continue to live in the tunnel. Most of the entrances have been padlocked or welded shut by Amtrak police. Many long–term residents have been informed they are trespassing and have been threatened with arrest. As this book goes to press, the tunnel residents have been notified that eviction is imminent.

Acknowledgments

The residents of the tunnel granted me the privilege of documenting their lives underground. I deeply appreciate their cooperation and trust.

Bernard Monte Isaac was my primary guide inside the tunnel between 1991 and 1995. Most often my visits were weekly. Bernard's patience and commitment to the project never ceased despite temperatures in the windswept tunnel that sometimes fell below zero. Extreme weather conditions became instead his opportunity to acquaint me with the survival skills necessary for residency in the tunnel. Bernard became my eyes when a flashlight could not penetrate the darkness, and his ears were always alert to the sound of approaching trains.

I will always be grateful.

Graffiti writers have painted the tunnel walls for decades, and I would like to acknowledge the work reproduced in this book. The final graffito of the late David Smith, known as "Sane," appears on page 13. It reads, Modern Day Society is guilty of intellectual terrorism..., a quotation by Bernard. Smith's brother, Roger, collaborated with graffiti writer Chris Pape to paint the Goya mural depicted on the same page. Bernard assisted with whitewashing the wall. Chris, whose tag is "Freedom," has painted murals for the tunnel residents since the early 1980s. His murals also appear on pages 50 and 51.

Background information for the prologue was culled from back issues of The New York Times; Carl W. Condit's The Port of New York; Robert Caro's The Power Broker; Rick Beard's collection, On Being Homeless: Historical Perspectives; Nels Anderson's "The Homeless in New York City," a 1934 report for the Welfare Council of New York; and Robert A. M. Stern, Gregory Gilmartin, and John Montague Massengale's New York 1900. Peter Derrick's encyclopedic knowledge of railroad history was also a valued resource. Kim Hopper visited New York City's underground homeless communities as early as 1979 and generously shared his experiences and historical research.

This book could not have been realized without the support of institutions and the advice and encouragement of colleagues and friends. Financial assistance arrived at a moment when it would have been impossible to continue without it. New York State Council on the Arts initially funded the project through an Individual Artist Grant in Architecture, Design, and Planning. As NYSCA grants administrator, the late Deborah Norden encouraged me to keep applying. The project was later sustained by a Visual Artist Fellowship grant in photography from the National Endowment for the Arts, a federal agency, and more recently by a grant from the Graham Foundation for Advanced Studies in the Fine Arts. I am grateful to John

Hill, Conrad Levenson, France Morin, Maren Stange, and Steve Zeitlin for their support. Bonnie Yochelson actively supported the tunnel project from its outset.

The Cooper Union School of Art provided ongoing support for the project. Jay Iselin and Beverly Wilson encouraged me to organize a symposium on homeless issues in 1992, which considerably broadened my perspective. Robert Rindler offered solutions to the sometimes overwhelming combination of full-time teaching responsibilities and artistic pursuits. Jacklynn Johnson transcribed most of the four years of audiotaped oral histories. Waldo Tejada provided translation. Lawrence Mirsky contributed to the organization of the design process. Jacqueline Kessler carefully formatted the pages and skillfully fine-tuned the typography. Lucy Leirião, a Cooper Union intern, worked cheerfully and tirelessly on many stages of the project. Jeffrey Piazza frequently arrived for the night shift. Yvette Amstelveen and Tiffani Casteel Replogle assisted in the early stages. Mindy Lang, Tom Romer, and Dmitry Krasny in the Center for Design and Typography also shared their expertise. Jameel Ahmad and the Cooper Union Research Foundation supported further development of the project.

Alan Trachtenberg thoughtfully read and responded to the preliminary manuscript. Georgette Ballance, William H. Knull III, Gloria Kury, Roger Schickedantz, Barbara Spackman, and Frank Gardner provided valuable input at later stages. Kai Erikson and Steve Zeitlin encouraged and advised the collection of oral histories. Larry Kenney at Yale University Press provided careful textual editing. Kathy Kennedy printed the gelatin silver prints.

I would especially like to acknowledge Judy Metro, my editor at Yale University Press, for her commitment to the project and for patiently guiding the book to completion.

The Architecture of Despair, *my ongoing photographic documentation of New York City homeless communities, began in 1989. Several colleagues and associates have encouraged my efforts over the past six years, and I gratefully acknowledge their generosity and support. Diana Balmori first brought my work to the attention of Yale University Press when we co–authored the book* Transitory Gardens, Uprooted Lives. *Simon Lowinsky and his staff at Lowinsky Gallery have provided support for my exhibitions since 1993. Charles Hobson has guided the development of my documentary projects. Mary Ellen Mark offered sound advice on several occasions. Patricia Colville, Stanley Greenberg, Yolanda C. Knull, E.J. Koster–Monteith, and Jerry Ordover also advised the project at many stages. John Dale, Mark Singer, Jennifer Toth, and Terry Williams are colleagues with whom I have shared experiences and concerns about underground homeless issues.*

I deeply appreciate the encouragement and support that my family and faithful friends have provided throughout the years.

Some of the tunnel residents are in desperate need. I am grateful to Mary Brosnahan and her staff at the Coalition for the Homeless, who have responded to every request with compassion, understanding, and solutions.

The Tunnel
was published by Yale University Press,
New Haven and London.
The text was edited by Judy Metro and
Lawrence Kenney, Yale University Press.
The book was designed by Margaret Morton.
Page composition was by Jacqueline Kessler,
assisted by Lucy Leirião, Cooper Union.

The typeface is Palatino, originally cut by
Herman Zapf in 1950. This updated Palatino
version was set with a Linotronic
computerized system.

The text paper is Condat Supreme Dull.
The endleaf paper is Rainbow Antique.
Production of the book was supervised by
Mary M. Mayer, Yale University Press.
The book was printed by Stinehour Press,
Lunenburg, Vermont, and bound by
The Riverside Group, Rochester, New York.

The oral histories were edited by
Margaret Morton from audiotaped interviews
conducted between 1991 and 1995.

Margaret Morton's photographs are courtesy
of Simon Lowinsky Gallery, New York City.